AMERICA AT WAR

THE AMERICAN REVOLUTIONARY WAR
1775–1783

Simon Rose

www.av2books.com

AV² provides enriched content that supplements and complements this book. Weigl's AV² books strive to create inspired learning and engage young minds in a total learning experience.

Your AV² Media Enhanced books come alive with...

Audio
Listen to sections of the book read aloud.

Key Words
Study vocabulary, and complete a matching word activity.

Video
Watch informative video clips.

Quizzes
Test your knowledge.

Go to **www.av2books.com,** and enter this book's unique code.

BOOK CODE

K 2 7 6 2 1 5

Embedded Weblinks
Gain additional information for research.

Slide Show
View images and captions, and prepare a presentation.

AV² by Weigl brings you media enhanced books that support active learning.

Try This!
Complete activities and hands-on experiments.

... and much, much more!

Published by AV² by Weigl
350 5th Avenue, 59th Floor
New York, NY 10118

Websites: www.av2books.com   www.weigl.com

Library of Congress Cataloging-in-Publication Data
Rose, Simon.
  American Revolutionary War / Simon Rose.
     pages cm. -- (America at war)
 Includes index.
  ISBN 978-1-4896-0512-2 (hardcover : alk. paper) -- ISBN 978-1-4896-0513-9 (softcover : alk. paper) -- ISBN 978-1-4896-0514-6 (ebk.) -- ISBN 978-1-4896-0515-3 (ebk.)
 1. United States--History--Revolution, 1775-1783--Juvenile literature. I. Title.
  E208.R65 2014
  973.3--dc23
                          2014017527

Printed in the United States of America in North Mankato, Minnesota
1 2 3 4 5 6 7 8 9 0 18 17 16 15 14

052014
WEP310514

Editor: Heather Kissock
Design: Mandy Christiansen

CONTENTS

America at War

The United States is a country that was born out of conflict. The American Revolutionary War was a fight for independence from **colonial rule**. From 1775 to 1783, colonists fought British rule for the right to forge their own destiny. Their commitment to the cause established the country as a fierce and loyal **ally**. When called upon, the United States has always fought bravely to protect its values and way of life.

The American Revolutionary War took place on land and at sea. Ships battled each other along the coast of North America as well as in European waters.

Since its inception, the United States has been involved in a number of wars and conflicts. These include the War of 1812, the American Civil War, the Mexican-American War, and several battles with American Indians. The United States was also involved in the latter stages of World War I and played a major role in World War II. Since 1945 alone, the United States has taken part in conflicts in Korea, Vietnam, Iraq, and Afghanistan.

No matter how a war ends, it usually leads to changes for both sides of the conflict. On the global scale, borders change, new countries are created, people win their freedom, and **dictators** are deposed. Changes also occur on a national level for almost every country involved.

The United States has experienced great change as a result of war. War has shaped the country's political, economic, and social landscape, making it the country it is today.

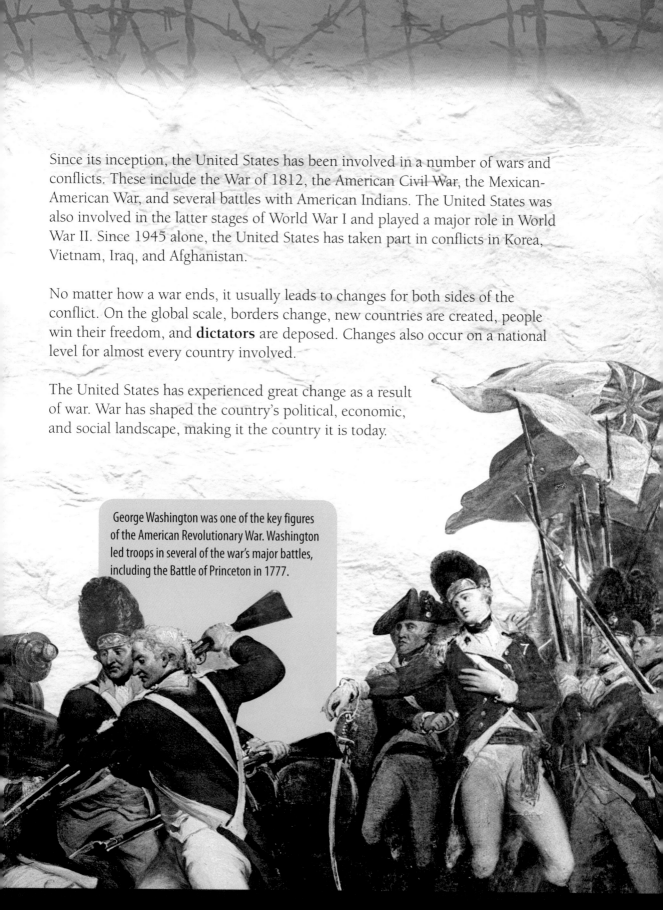

George Washington was one of the key figures of the American Revolutionary War. Washington led troops in several of the war's major battles, including the Battle of Princeton in 1777.

A War Begins

Tensions had been simmering for a while in the American **colonies**. Since the **French and Indian War** ended in 1763, the British government had been taking extreme steps to rebuild its economy, which had been drained due to the war effort. Many of the decisions being made had a direct impact on the colonists. The British government implemented rules about where colonists could live, how they could ship goods, and to whom they could sell these goods. It also introduced heavy taxes on commonly used products, such as tea and sugar.

The colonists were growing increasingly frustrated with the decisions Great Britain was making on their behalf. Many started rebelling openly against British rule. Conflicts between colonists and British soldiers often became violent. One of the best-known events occurred on March 5, 1770, when British soldiers fired into a group of protestors. Five people were killed and another six were wounded in what is now known as the Boston Massacre.

In May 1773, Great Britain introduced the Tea Act. This gave the East India Company a **monopoly** on selling tea directly to the colonies. The monopoly meant that American merchants could not buy tea from anyone else. They had no choice but to pay the price the company offered, including taxes. To show their opposition to the Tea Act, on December 16, 1773, a group of colonists boarded three ships in Boston Harbor and dumped 342 chests of tea into the water. This later became known as the Boston Tea Party.

The Boston Massacre occurred when a group of colonists met at the Customs House to protest the British occupation of their city.

Roots of the American Revolutionary War

AMERICAN EXPANSION

As a result of the French and Indian War, Great Britain gained control of territory between the Mississippi River and the Appalachian Mountains. Most of the American Indians in this area had fought against Great Britain in the war. In order to maintain good relations with the American Indians and keep peace in the area, King George III of England issued a Royal Proclamation in October 1763 that prevented American colonists from settling in the lands west of the Appalachians. This angered the colonists, and many simply ignored the new boundary.

THE ENLIGHTENMENT

From the late 17th century and throughout the 18th century, Europe went through a period called the **Enlightenment**. This period brought new ideas about the way countries should be governed. English philosopher John Locke believed that government was meant to serve the people and that everyone had a natural right to life, liberty, and property. He also believed that governments should have a system of checks and balances. American colonists were heavily influenced by this approach to government, especially when faced with new British taxes and laws.

TAXATION

To recover the costs of the French and Indian War, the British government imposed several new taxes. The Sugar Act of 1764 imposed taxes on non-British goods that were imported from the Caribbean, such as sugar and molasses. The Stamp Act placed a tax on all printed materials. In 1767, the Townshend Revenue Acts placed new taxes on popular items such as glass, paper, and tea. The colonists felt that they should not be taxed if they were not represented in the British Parliament, arguing that there should be "no taxation without representation."

NEW LAWS FOR THE LAND

The British government also implemented a series of laws that were meant to save money. In 1764, the government passed the Currency Act, which banned the colonies from issuing paper currency. All colonies had to use the British pound instead. Any paper money in the hands of colonists lost its value. Their savings were ruined as a result. In early 1765, the Quartering Act ordered colonists to provide food and housing for British soldiers. This put a further toll on people already facing financial hardship.

A War of Independence

The American Revolutionary War began as a dispute between Great Britain and the Thirteen Colonies in North America. The colonies wanted to run their own affairs and declared independence. Although the war began as a regional conflict, it had a global impact. France, Spain, and the Netherlands gave support to the new United States and fought against Great Britain at sea, in Europe, in the Caribbean, and in India. France and Spain also sent troops to fight in North America. At the end of the war, the United States achieved independence and became a major world power over the next century.

This map shows the scope of the war and the key battles that took place.

NEW
SPAIN

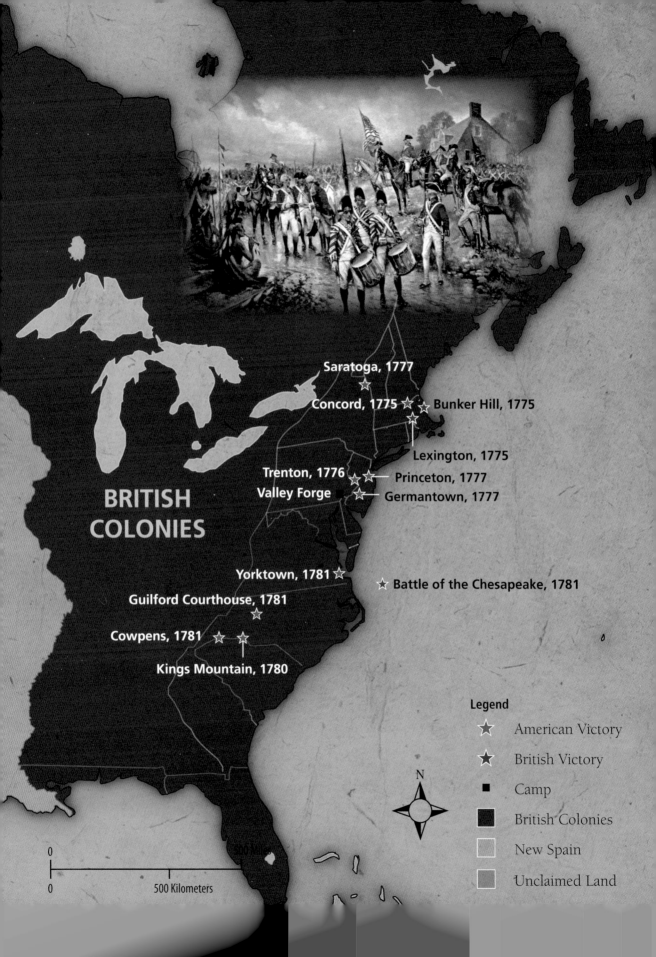

Saratoga, 1777

Concord, 1775 ☆ ☆ Bunker Hill, 1775

Lexington, 1775

Trenton, 1776 ☆ ☆ — Princeton, 1777
Valley Forge ☆ — Germantown, 1777

BRITISH
COLONIES

Yorktown, 1781 ☆   ☆ Battle of the Chesapeake, 1781

Guilford Courthouse, 1781 ☆

Cowpens, 1781 ☆ ☆
Kings Mountain, 1780

N

Legend

☆ American Victory

☆ British Victory

■ Camp

◼ British Colonies

◻ New Spain

◻ Unclaimed Land

0
0   500 Kilometers

The Colonies Go to War

The British government reacted strongly to the escalating colonist rebellion. In an attempt to exert its power over the colonists, it introduced the Coercive Acts in March 1774. Also known as the Intolerable Acts, the new laws closed Boston Harbor until the East India Company was compensated for the tea destroyed during the Boston Tea Party. Massachusetts was also placed under direct British military control, with General Thomas Gage appointed as the governor. Another edict, the Quebec Act, extended Quebec's borders to the Ohio River. This blocked some of the colonies from expanding to the west.

The year after the war began, the Second Continental Congress met in Philadelphia to draft the Declaration of Independence, which formalized the colonies' separation from Great Britain.

The colonies knew they had to band together if they wanted the situation to change. In September 1774, the First Continental Congress met in Philadelphia. Made up of delegates from most of the colonies, the group gathered to discuss the British government's actions and decide on a course of action. Although the delegates did not yet support independence, they protested against what they considered to be unjust laws and taxes. After the meeting, they issued a declaration about the rights of citizens.

The dissent continued to escalate over the next year. In April 1775, British officials ordered General Gage to seize all weapons and gunpowder being stockpiled by the colonists. Approximately 700 soldiers were sent to the weapons depots at Lexington and Concord, where they destroyed the colonists' military supplies. However, during their march back to Boston, the British came under attack by the local **militia** and suffered approximately 250 **casualties**. News of the fighting spread quickly, and colonial forces converged on Boston to begin a **siege** of the city. On May 10, the Second Continental Congress of all 13 colonies met in Philadelphia. The delegates appointed George Washington as commander-in-chief of the new Continental Army. On June 17, the Battle of Bunker Hill became the first major engagement of the war. Although the British won the battle, they suffered more than 1,000 casualties. The colonists were encouraged and began to grow in confidence as the war continued.

George Washington
The First U.S. President

George Washington was born in Westmoreland County, Virginia, in 1732, as the son of a wealthy tobacco planter. His first experience as a soldier came during the French and Indian War. After the war, Washington took over his family's estate at Mount Vernon. He was elected to the Virginia legislature in 1758. Washington became a leading figure in the opposition to British rule in North America. He was one of Virginia's delegates at the First and Second Continental Congresses and was appointed as commander-in-chief of the Continental Army in May 1775.

Washington gave up command of the army in 1783 and retired to Mount Vernon, but was soon involved in the **Constitutional Convention** in Philadelphia. He was elected as the first president of the United States in 1789. Washington served two terms and stepped down after eight years in office. He once again retired to Mount Vernon, where he died in December 1799 at the age of 67.

George Washington took his oath of office on April 30, 1789, at Federal Hall in New York City. New York was the national capital at the time.

Mount Vernon is located about 16 miles (25.7 km) south of Washington, DC, in the state of Virginia. Today, it is one of the most visited historic estates in the country.

Americans Who Served in the Revolutionary War

The American Revolutionary War brought together colonists from various backgrounds. Whether rich or poor, black or white, people united together to fight against the repression of the British government. Most men were soldiers in the Continental Army, but some were members of forces recruited from the militias of the individual colonies and local communities. Sailors served mostly on ships along the east coast and in the Atlantic Ocean. Americans also spent time as prisoners of war, where they often experienced harsh conditions.

Soldiers

American armies were small compared to the European armies of the time. The largest army commanded in the field by Washington was estimated to have only about 17,000 men. At the beginning of the war, soldiers only enlisted for short periods of time. This was lengthened as the war continued. Soldiers were mostly young men between the ages of 18 and 24. Many soldiers were from the poorest levels of society. Volunteering for military service usually meant promises of cash payments or of land, once the Americans won the war.

Prior to the war, the colonies did not have a professional army. As a result, most of the men who joined the Continental Army lacked the experience and discipline of the British Army's professional soldiers. This situation changed as the war progressed. As leader of the Continental Army, George Washington developed training programs and enlisted the help of professional soldiers from allied armed forces. Training greatly improved during the winter of 1777 to 1778, when the Continental Army set up camp at Valley Forge, Pennsylvania. The efforts made during this time contributed to the American successes in the later years of the war.

George Washington relied on a Prussian officer, Baron Friedrich von Steuben, to assist in training his soldiers at Valley Forge. Von Steuben is credited with turning the untrained troops into skilled soldiers.

The minutemen were a specialized force whose members were pulled from militia units. Minutemen were named for their ability to enter battle at a moment's notice. They were often the first troops called to fight.

Militia

The militia was made up of local citizens who were willing to defend their colony when needed. When the Continental Army was formed, some militia members left their local units to join the larger force. Others remained with their militia units and fought under their own local commanders. Lower ranking militia officers often had little tactical knowledge, although higher-ranking officers may have had previous experience serving in the French and Indian War.

Although they would only serve for short periods and were reluctant to travel too far from home, militia soldiers proved effective against the larger and more experienced British Army. The heavily forested areas of North America were not always suitable for European-style warfare, where soldiers could advance in lines and fight side by side. Militia soldiers would attack the British from hiding places and then retreat to take up new positions. This led to many British casualties in the war's early battles. Militia soldiers often served as **snipers** and also played a leading role in the American successes in the South later in the war. In some colonies, the militia helped maintain local law and order and defend against American Indian raids, which were encouraged by the British.

Sailors

When the war began, the British had an obvious advantage over the Americans. Besides foot soldiers, the British also had a navy. The Americans realized that they would have to add a naval component to their own military effort. They founded the Continental Navy in 1775 so that they could wage war at sea as well as on land. The British Royal Navy had more than 250 ships, so the Americans were greatly outnumbered. The Americans realized that good strategy would be key to a victory on the water. Their aim was to disrupt British operations at sea and intercept ships carrying supplies to the British Army in North America. Although the Continental Navy had fewer ships, American sailors were just as skilled as their British counterparts. American ships operated in North American, European, and British waters.

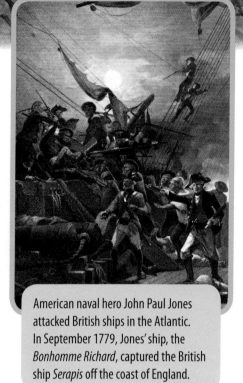

American naval hero John Paul Jones attacked British ships in the Atlantic. In September 1779, Jones' ship, the *Bonhomme Richard*, captured the British ship *Serapis* off the coast of England.

The small Continental Navy had little effect on the war effort, but many sailors served on the ships of U.S. privateers. These were private ships that the U.S. government authorized to attack foreign vessels during wartime. More than 50,000 sailors served with privateers and caused great damage to British ships. During the war, at least 1,500 ships were operated by privateers, and more than 2,000 British ships were captured.

The Continental Navy performed raids on British properties in other parts of the world. In March 1776, a fleet of ships sailed into the Bahamas to take possession of weapons and ammunition stored there by the British.

Marines

To support their newly formed Continental Navy, the Continental Congress announced the formation of two corps of marines in November 1775. The Continental Marines were to serve as landing forces for the navy. While sailors stayed on their ships to fight, the marines operated on both land and sea. They often continued a battle that had moved from water to land.

Similar to the Army, many of the marines who enlisted in the Continental Navy came from marine corps that had already been established in individual colonies. Over the course of the war, more than 2,000 men enlisted in the Marines.

Today's U.S. Marine Corps traces its roots to the Continental Marines.

PRISONERS OF WAR

The British government regarded Continental soldiers as traitors. When captured, most were forced to endure difficult conditions. The British housed many captives in prison ships. These ships were overcrowded and unsanitary. American prisoners usually received fewer rations than British soldiers. With no fruit or fresh vegetables, the prisoners suffered from scurvy, a disease that causes bleeding gums and loose teeth. Prisoners also suffered from other diseases, including dysentery, smallpox, and yellow fever. It is estimated that more than 8,500 Americans may have died as prisoners of war. This exceeds the number of deaths on the battlefield.

A Soldier's Uniform

HEADGEAR

Soldiers wore a three-cornered hat called a tricorne. This type of hat was popular in the late 18th century. A circular or oval knot of ribbons called a cockade could be worn on one side of the hat. This indicated an officer's rank and his allegiance. Most hats were made of wool felt or beaver fur and dyed black or white.

As the Continental Army had only just been formed, the uniforms worn by soldiers and militia members often varied. In fact, most soldiers wore their everyday clothes. Some militia members, however, had actual uniforms that indicated a united fighting force. As the war progressed, efforts were made to standardize the clothing worn by soldiers.

JACKETS AND COATS

Brown was adopted as the original uniform color for the Continental Army in 1775, but there was a shortage of brown cloth. In 1779, George Washington chose a blue uniform with a red trim on the lapels, cuffs, and collar for his soldiers. This distinguished them from the British soldiers, who wore red uniforms. Coats were mostly made of wool, but linen, velvet, silk, or fabric blends were also used. The coat was either mid-thigh or knee length and was worn over a shirt and a waistcoat made of linen or wool.

SHIRTS

Soldiers wore a long, loose-fitting shirt called a hunting shirt. This was pulled on over the head and only had buttons at the top. The shirt was made of linen or cotton. Some had ruffles at the wrist or at the chest.

TROUSERS AND STOCKINGS

Trousers and breeches were usually white and made of cotton, linen, wool, or fabric blends. They could extend just below the calf or down to the ankle. Trousers were usually looser than breeches and had adjustable waistbands. Stockings were worn with both trousers and breeches. They stretched above the knee and were secured with garters. Stockings were usually white and made of wool, cotton, linen, silk, or fabric blends.

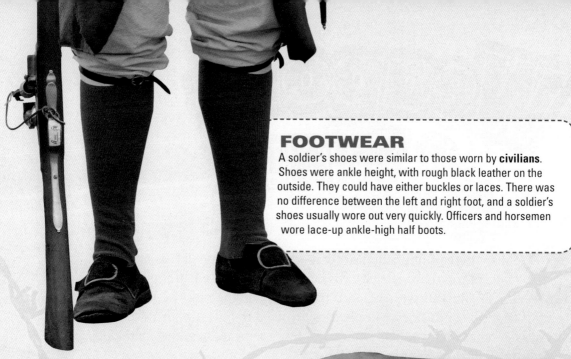

FOOTWEAR

A soldier's shoes were similar to those worn by **civilians**. Shoes were ankle height, with rough black leather on the outside. They could have either buckles or laces. There was no difference between the left and right foot, and a soldier's shoes usually wore out very quickly. Officers and horsemen wore lace-up ankle-high half boots.

KNAPSACK

A soldier's knapsack carried his spare clothing and toiletry articles, including a razor for shaving, a mirror, and a comb. It would also hold candleholders and a tinderbox with steel and flint so that the soldier could start a fire. Some soldiers had a fishhook and some twine to catch fish, in case they camped near a lake or river.

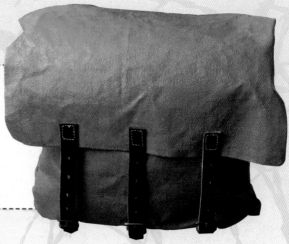

CANTEEN

Three different types of canteens were used to carry drinking water. The militia mostly used canteens that were shaped like a small keg. Some of the regular soldiers carried pewter canteens, which were kept in their knapsacks or haversacks. The most common canteen looked like a small wooden barrel with a wooden plug. These canteens had a carrying strap that was placed over the right shoulder so that the canteen rested on the soldier's left hip.

Weapons of War

Soldiers in the Continental Army relied on weapons such as muskets, rifles, pistols, bayonets, swords, and cannons when battling the British. Muskets with attached bayonets were the most frequently used weapons by both sides. Most battles involved the two opposing armies facing each other over a wide distance and firing repeatedly at the enemy, before advancing for closer combat.

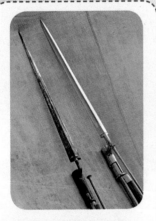

MUSKETS

The most important weapon of the Revolutionary War was the flintlock musket. This was a muzzle-loaded, single shot, smoothbore gun, fired from the shoulder. The weapon fired round lead balls. The standard rate of fire was three shots per minute. Flintlock muskets were most accurate at a range between 60 and 80 yards (55 and 73 meters). This meant that men had to be quite close to each other during a battle.

BAYONETS

The bayonet was a long knife that was fastened to the end of a soldier's musket. The blade ranged from 14 to 30 inches (36 to 76 centimeters) in length. Bayonets were used to stab the enemy when fighting at close range. They were useful when engaging in hand-to-hand combat and during a charge. A bayonet charge at the right point during a battle could be very effective in making the enemy retreat.

RIFLES

Rifles had a longer barrel than muskets. They also had a longer range and were much more accurate. However, rifles did not have bayonets and took longer to load. Rifles were used to their best effect by snipers. British officers were often advised to remove distinctive markings from their uniforms so that they would not be easy targets for American sharpshooters.

PISTOLS

While many soldiers brought their personal pistols to war, they were not the weapon of choice. For the most part, they were carried by officers and used sparingly. Pistols were not considered an effective weapon due to their long loading time. Soldiers had to reload after each shot was taken, leaving them vulnerable to attack. Pistols were also not very accurate at long range. They were used mainly in close combat.

SWORDS

Officers had a variety of swords at their disposal. **Cavalry** officers relied on sabers, which were heavy swords with curved blades and one cutting edge. The officers could swing them at the enemy from their horses. Some officers also carried small, straight sabers. These were often used to direct soldiers in battle. **Infantry** soldiers sometimes carried hanger swords or cutlasses. These were short and wide slashing swords.

CANNONS

The cannons used in the war were mostly 3, 4, or 6-pound (1.4, 1.8, or 2.7 kilogram) guns that were mounted on wooden carriages with large wheels on either side. The guns were very heavy, and up to 14 men were needed to operate them. Cannons fired solid balls or different types of small shot. They also fired shells. These hollow iron balls were filled with gunpowder and lit with a fuse. The guns had a range between 1,000 and 2,000 yards (914 and 1,829 m) and were very useful weapons for the Americans in such battles as Bunker Hill and Yorktown. The guns were difficult to use in heavy rain because the gunpowder needed to be kept dry.

Timeline

The War on the Battlefield

January 3, 1777
Washington wins the
Battle of Princeton.

April 19, 1775
The first fighting takes place
between American and British
troops at Lexington and Concord.

June 17, 1775
The Battle of Bunker Hill
takes place during the
Siege of Boston. The
British win the battle but
suffer heavy casualties.

**December 25
to 26, 1776**
Washington crosses
the Delaware River and
captures Trenton.

The War at Home

September 5, 1774
The First Continental
Congress meets in
Philadelphia. The colonies
discuss acting together to
resist what they consider
to be unfair British laws
and taxes.

May 10, 1775
The Second Continental
Congress meets in
Philadelphia to organize
the war efforts and
begins to make plans
for independence.

December 19, 1777
The Continental Army gathers at Valley Forge, Pennsylvania, where it spends the winter and prepares for battle the following June.

October 7, 1780
Patriot militia defeat **Loyalist** militia at the Battle of Kings Mountain, forcing General Cornwallis to abandon plans for a British invasion of North Carolina.

October 17, 1777
American forces defeat General Burgoyne at the Second Battle of Saratoga.

October 4, 1777
The Americans are defeated at the Battle of Germantown.

October 19, 1781
Cornwallis surrenders the British Army at Yorktown. This is the last major battle of the war.

July 4, 1776
The Thirteen Colonies adopt the Declaration of Independence.

September 3, 1783
The **Treaty** of Paris officially ends the American Revolutionary War.

Key Battles

I n the early years of the Revolutionary War, American forces had few victories against the British Army. Over time, however, the American forces steadily improved, and they began to win more battles. Not only did these victories raise morale, they also attracted the support of other countries. France, in particular, formed an alliance with the United States and sent both troops and ships to North America. French support was crucial to the British defeat at Yorktown in October 1781, which effectively ended the war.

The British Army acquired the Hessians from German princes, who kept private armies to protect their lands. Most of the soldiers were not paid for their efforts. The money paid for their services went directly to the prince.

Battles of Trenton and Princeton

In the late fall of 1776, the Continental Army suffered several defeats around New York City. Washington's soldiers retreated across New Jersey and into Pennsylvania. Morale was low. Desertions from the army were increasing, and troops were short of supplies and ill-equipped to face the coming winter. When Washington received reinforcements in late December, he decided to boost morale by staging another attack against British forces.

The target was the **garrison** of **Hessians** in nearby Trenton, New Jersey. On December 26, facing rain, sleet, and snow, Washington crossed the Delaware River with his forces. The Hessians had about 1,500 men to face the 2,400 Americans. The American attack on Trenton began at about 8:00 am, from different directions. The Hessians were no match for the Americans. Some of the Hessians managed to escape, but more than 900 were taken prisoner.

DECEMBER 26

George Washington leads his army into the town of Trenton and stages an attack against 1,500 Hessians. The battle ends within an hour with the Hessian defeat.

JANUARY 2

British General Cornwallis and his men arrive in Trenton and attack the American forces at Trenton. Theses attacks are unsuccessful.

The British soon sent reinforcements, led by General Charles Cornwallis, to attack Washington's forces. On January 2, Cornwallis launched three unsuccessful attacks against the American positions. The next day, Washington moved his army and attacked British forces based in Princeton, New Jersey. Although some of the British soldiers managed to get away and rejoin Cornwallis' main force, others continued battling the Americans. However, it was not long before they surrendered.

One of the best-known paintings about the American Revolutionary War is *Washington Crossing the Delaware* by Emanuel Leutze, which shows the commander preparing for his attack on the Hessians at Trenton.

Washington considered continuing his attack against the other British bases in New Jersey, but was wary of Cornwallis' nearby army. He decided to move his army to northern New Jersey and establish winter quarters there, in the safety of American-held land. The Battles of Trenton and Princeton were only small engagements, but they had a major effect on the war. They proved that Americans could defeat the British Army. Morale among the troops improved, and more men enlisted in the Continental Army.

JANUARY 3

Washington moves his army to Princeton, New Jersey, and battles the British forces there. The battle is another victory for U.S. forces.

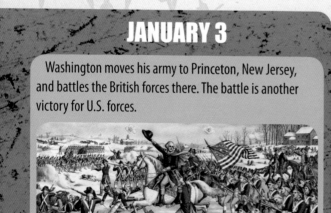

JANUARY 3

Washington decides against another battle and moves his army to New Jersey for the winter.

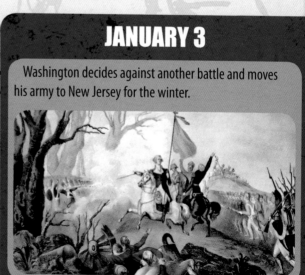

Battles of Saratoga

Early in 1777, the British devised a plan to isolate New England, separating the heart of the rebellion from the other colonies. The plan involved the cooperation of three separate units. General John Burgoyne was to move his forces from Quebec down the Hudson River. Another British force, led by General Barrimore St. Leger, would move east from Lake Ontario. A third British army, under General William Howe, would march north from New York. Together, they were to meet in the city of Albany and move toward the Hudson River Valley, where they would attack the American force's northern army.

The plan seemed sound, but soon ran into problems. Most of St. Leger's force had to turn back after skirmishes with American forces. Howe decided to have his army attack Philadelphia instead. Burgoyne's arrival was delayed by American forces who blocked his route. He did not arrive in the area until mid-September. Since he was getting very low on supplies, Burgoyne decided to try to capture Albany before winter.

Burgoyne had a distinguished career before the war. He was elected to the British parliament in 1761 and was also a noted playwright.

The British and American forces met at Freeman's Farm near Saratoga, New York, on September 19. The British attacked, but American riflemen killed many of the British officers in the advance party. The Americans then charged, but ran into Burgoyne's main army and were forced back. Fierce fighting took place all afternoon, before the Americans withdrew. Although the British secured the area, they suffered more than 600 casualties.

SEPTEMBER 19

British and American forces battle at Freeman's Farm, near Saratoga. The British secure the area, but are unable to advance their line.

OCTOBER 7

Burgoyne leads his forces on a **reconnaissance** mission to see how best to attack the American position. The British troops come under American attack.

Burgoyne decided to hold his position in the hope that reinforcements would arrive from New York City. When his supplies had run dangerously low and he realized that help might not be coming, Burgoyne met with his commanders. They decided to send soldiers to check if an attack on the American left flank might be possible. Burgoyne led a force of about 1,500 men to scout the area and prepare for battle. While on their reconnaissance mission, however, the British troops were attacked by American forces. The British had no choice but to retreat to fortified positions near Freeman's Farm. Burgoyne had lost about 600 men in the battle. After contemplating fighting his way north, he opened negotiations with the Americans, led by General Horatio Gates. On October 17, almost 6,000 British troops surrendered.

Battles of Saratoga

Freeman's Farm

Wheatfield

Main Attack

Mill Creek

Hudson River

Mill Creek

Hudson River

Bemis Heights

■ British Troops
→ British Movements
■ American Troops
→ American Movements

0 _____ 1
Scale of Miles

Saratoga was a turning point in the American Revolutionary War. The American victory persuaded France to enter the war and provide support to the American forces. This support would be crucial to the final outcome of the war.

OCTOBER 8

The British begin their retreat to their fortified position by Freeman's Farm. They are soon surrounded by American forces.

OCTOBER 17

The British forces surrender to the Americans. As part of the surrender agreement, the British troops are allowed to return to Great Britain, provided they do not rejoin the war.

Battle of Yorktown

In 1778, France signed an alliance with the Americans, agreeing to help them in their fight against the British. In July 1780, more than 5,000 French troops landed in Rhode Island, and the French Navy soon had a large number of ships in North American waters. The American strategy was to launch an attack on New York City. The French commander, however, persuaded Washington to strike farther south. In August, the French and American forces began moving south to Yorktown, Virginia. Here, they were to confront Cornwallis' army of about 8,000 men. French ships then moved into position along the coast to prevent the British Army from being resupplied or escaping. By late September, the British forces were trapped.

Washington had about 17,600 American and French troops. Seriously outnumbered, Cornwallis repositioned his forces, bringing troops from outlying posts to fortified lines closer to the town. Washington also began moving his forces and set up **artillery** to begin bombarding the British. Both sides exchanged fire while the preparations were being made.

The French forces were commanded by Jean Baptiste Donatien de Vimeur, the Count of Rochambeau. Rochambeau brought approximately 40 years of battle experience to the war and provided Washington with valuable advice in planning the Yorktown battle.

OCTOBER 9

After weeks of preparation, George Washington fires the first shot in the Battle of Yorktown. The French and American forces begin their bombardment of the British.

OCTOBER 14

Colonel Alexander Hamilton leads a force of American and French soldiers to capture two British fortified positions.

On October 9, Washington personally fired the first shot, and the battle officially began. The French and Americans bombarded the British lines for three days. On October 14, American Colonel Alexander Hamilton attacked and captured two of the British fortified positions. The British then attacked the American and French lines on October 16. They managed to disable some of the guns and took some prisoners, but were not able to break through the lines. Cornwallis then made his own attempt at breaking through the American lines. He tried to move some troops across the York River to Gloucester Point, but the operation failed due to bad weather.

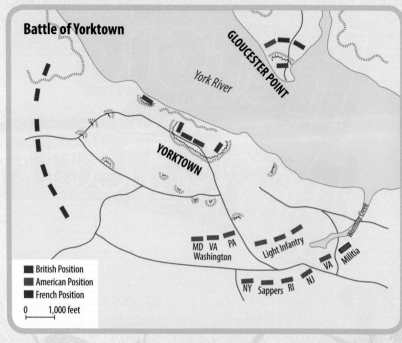

Battle of Yorktown

GLOUCESTER POINT

York River

YORKTOWN

Wormley Creek

MD VA PA
Washington

Light Infantry

VA Militia

NY Sappers RI NJ

■ British Position
■ American Position
■ French Position

0   1,000 feet

By this time, Cornwallis was almost out of ammunition. With no sign of help in sight, he realized that his situation was hopeless. He approached the Americans and opened negotiations. On October 19, he and his 8,000 British soldiers surrendered.

OCTOBER 16

The British counterattack the American and French lines. Although they have some success, they are unable to break the American lines.

OCTOBER 19

General Cornwallis and his soldiers surrender to the American forces.

Heroic Americans

The men who served in the American Revolutionary War came from a range of backgrounds. They shared a common desire to fight for their country's freedom and independence. While many performed heroic acts, as the war progressed, some names became better known than others. Some soldiers were hailed for their bravery and strong leadership. Others were celebrated because they performed feats unlike anyone else.

Nathanael Greene
(1742–1786)

Nathanael Greene was one of the leading generals of the Revolutionary War. He was born in Rhode Island in 1742. Elected to the Rhode Island legislature in 1770, Greene soon became a supporter of the American colonies declaring independence from Great Britain. In 1774, Greene helped to form a Rhode Island militia unit called the Kentish Guards and later commanded the Rhode Island militia. In 1775, he became a brigadier general in the Continental Army.

In late 1780, Washington appointed Greene to command American forces in the South. The army had suffered heavy defeats at the hands of the British forces. Greene knew he could not defeat the British in a major battle but waged a successful campaign with small-scale actions. By the fall of 1781, the British were only in control of the cities of Savannah and Charleston, which they left in 1782.

After the war, Greene lived on the Mulberry Grove estate in Georgia, where he died in 1786 at the age of 43.

Daniel Morgan
(1736–1802)

Daniel Morgan was one of the most talented American generals during the Revolutionary War. Born in Hunterdon County, New Jersey, in 1736, he held a number of jobs before joining the British Army and serving in the French and Indian War. After the conflict, Morgan became a prominent citizen of Virginia. At the start of the Revolutionary War, he was placed in command of a Virginia rifle regiment and fought at the siege of Boston.

Over time, Morgan was promoted to the rank of colonel and joined Washington's main army. He fought in the Saratoga campaign and was later given command of troops in the South in late 1780. He led his troops to victory over the British at the Battle of Cowpens in January 1781.

Following the war, Morgan became a successful businessman in Virginia. After a brief return to military service in 1794, he served one term in Congress. Morgan died in Winchester, Virginia, in 1802, at the age of 66.

Henry Knox
(1750–1806)

Henry Knox served as a general in the Revolutionary War. He was one of George Washington's closest advisors and established training for artillerymen during the conflict.

Knox was born in Boston, Massachusetts, in 1750. When the Revolutionary War began, he first joined the Boston Grenadier Corps and then the Continental Army. Knox was appointed to command the Continental Regiment of Artillery and fought at the Battles of Bunker Hill, Long Island, Trenton, and Princeton. He was then promoted to brigadier general. At Yorktown, Knox's artillery was decisive in forcing the British surrender in October 1781.

Knox served as U.S. secretary of state for war from 1789 to 1794. He died in Thomaston, Maine, in October 1806 at the age of 56. The cities of Knoxville in Tennessee and Maine, and Fort Knox in Kentucky are named after him.

The Home Front

While the focus of the war was often on the soldiers and the fighting, many other people were affected by the conflict. Women, for instance, played an important role in keeping the local economy working and providing supplies for American troops. Many African Americans used the confusion of the war to escape from slavery. Not all of the colonists supported the war. Up to 20 percent of the population remained loyal to Great Britain and, as a result, had property confiscated or were harshly treated during the war. The conflict also caused economic disruption and led to great hardship throughout the colonies.

Women in the Revolutionary War

In the late 18th century, women worked very hard in the home. They cooked meals, made clothes and other household items, and brought up their children. Once the men left to join the war, there was even more work to do at home. Women were left to keep the family farm or business running while the war was going on. When the colonists began **boycotting** British goods, American women supported the use of items produced locally. In fact, many of them began producing some of the goods required. Some women formed sewing circles, where they produced a material called homespun. This material replaced the need for British textiles. Sewing circles also contributed directly to the war effort. When George Washington asked for clothing for his troops, women produced thousands of linen shirts.

Some women chose not to stay at home. Instead, they joined their husbands or male relatives at the Continental Army camps. Here, they helped with cooking, laundry, and nursing. Some women worked as spies, passing on vital information to Washington's army about British troop movements. A woman named Deborah Sampson disguised herself as a man and served in the Continental Army for a year. She fought in several battles before being honorably discharged in 1783.

Mary Ludwig Hays McCauly is one of the best-known women of the American Revolutionary War. Nicknamed Molly Pitcher, she brought water to cool the cannons and helped load them when needed.

African Americans and American Indians

African Americans, whether they were free or slaves, fought on both sides during the war. When the war started, no racial distinction was made regarding who was allowed to enlist. However, when George Washington became commander of the Continental Army, he banned African Americans from enlisting. The ban was not lifted until 1777, when the Continental Army was in need of more soldiers. The British, on the other hand, encouraged African Americans to enlist. In 1775, Dunmore's Proclamation was issued, offering freedom to slaves that joined the British Army. Over the course of the war, thousands of African Americans signed up on each side, all hoping to be awarded freedom when the war came to an end.

Crispus Attucks was a Patriot living in Boston. He became the war's first casualty when he was shot during the Boston Massacre.

Most of the American Indians east of the Mississippi River tried to stay out of the fighting. Many were worried about what would happen if the colonists won, since the British government had always protected American Indian lands from being taken by settlers. American Indians mostly sided with Great Britain during the war or took action against American forces on their own.

Some American Indians fought alongside U.S. forces. They served as scouts for the Continental Army, locating enemy positions and finding travel routes.

Loyalists

The Loyalists believed that the colonies would be better off remaining under British rule. They felt that the colonies would face an uncertain future if they no longer had the protection of the British Empire. Those who were in business had strong ties to Great Britain and knew how important trade with the mother country was to the colonial economy. Other Loyalists were simply afraid of the prospect of fighting the powerful British Army.

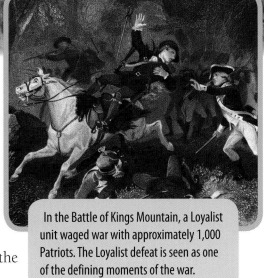

In the Battle of Kings Mountain, a Loyalist unit waged war with approximately 1,000 Patriots. The Loyalist defeat is seen as one of the defining moments of the war.

As the war went on, life became difficult for the Loyalists. The British Army could not always protect Loyalists living in areas controlled by Patriots. Many Loyalists had their property confiscated, lost their businesses, were imprisoned, or sometimes even killed. New York City was a Loyalist stronghold during the war, and there was also strong Loyalist support in parts of Georgia and South Carolina. After the war, many Loyalists moved to Canada. Some returned to Great Britain. The British government offered them compensation for their war losses. However, the money provided was usually far less than the amount the Loyalists had lost by giving up their businesses and homes in the colonies.

Loyalists faced abuse and humiliation for their support of British forces. One form of abuse was being tarred and feathered.

The Economy

The American colonies enjoyed prosperity in the years leading up to the Revolutionary War. They exported goods to Great Britain, Europe, and the Caribbean. As the colonists grew more prosperous, they imported food products and manufactured goods. In the second half of the 18th century, trade between the colonies also increased. The outbreak of war caused great disruption to the local economy. The British Royal Navy attacked or captured American merchant ships, and American ports were **blockaded**. Those who depended on imported goods became unemployed, and many products were in short supply. Labor shortages were common as more men left their jobs to join the fighting.

The poor value of the American currency led people to use the expression "not worth a Continental" when referring to useless items.

The war was very expensive. As the government was unable to raise taxes to pay for the war, it decided to print paper money. Called Continentals, the notes were little more than pieces of paper. While they were issued in dollar denominations, their worth was dependent on future tax **revenues** and was not backed up with any tangible assets. The government issued about $250 million in Continentals. This quantity created more problems for the economy. With so much money in circulation, **inflation** resulted. People had used their gold and silver to buy paper money that was ultimately of no value. By the end of the war, many Americans were in significant debt.

The War Comes to an End

The Americans won the Battle of Kings Mountain in October 1780 and in December, Nathanael Greene was given command of American forces in the South. On January 17, 1781, at the Battle of Cowpens in South Carolina, Daniel Morgan defeated a British army led by Banastre Tarleton. The tide of the war was beginning to turn in favor of the Americans, but they still faced very strong British forces.

The British won a series of battles, but Greene was steadily wearing Cornwallis' army down. In March, the British defeated Greene at the Battle of Guilford Courthouse, but sustained heavy casualties. Cornwallis retreated to get reinforcements and stock up on supplies before moving into Virginia. He decided to fortify Yorktown. Its proximity to the sea meant that it could be quickly resupplied by the Royal Navy. The sea also provided the army with an escape route, if under siege.

The Battle of Cowpens took place on January 17, 1781, in South Carolina. It was named for the pastures in which the fighting took place.

The British forces were outnumbered at Guilford Court House, with only 1,900 soldiers compared to more than 4,000 on the Patriot side.

In August, Washington began moving his combined American and French forces to Yorktown. On September 15, the French fleet defeated the British at the Battle of the Chesapeake. This battle effectively cut off Cornwallis from the Royal Navy. No supplies could get into Yorktown, and no British could leave. All the British could do was lay in wait of the American attack.

Washington and his army began the siege of Yorktown on September 28. After several days of bombardment, Cornwallis surrendered his army, which numbered approximately 8,000 men, on October 19. Yorktown was the last major battle of the war, but Great Britain still controlled some areas, such as Charleston, Savannah, and New York. British forces were eventually withdrawn from these areas, and the war officially came to an end with the signing of the Treaty of Paris.

The Battle of the Chesapeake lasted for only about two and a half hours, but it was turning point in the war and ultimately led to Cornwallis' surrender at Yorktown.

The Aftermath

The peace treaty that ended the war established the United States as an independent nation. In the years that followed, the newly-formed country took the steps necessary to develop a system of government and an American way of life. Other countries took note of the autonomy the war had given the United States. In Europe especially, citizens began reacting against traditional rule. Rebellions toppled governments and redefined the role of the people in the political process.

The Treaty of Paris

The Treaty of Paris was signed on September 3, 1783, following months of negotiations. Under the terms of the treaty, Great Britain recognized the independence of the United States. The Americans agreed to let the British forces leave North America peacefully and to pay all debts still owed to the British government. The United States gained territory in the west, with the British giving up control of all lands between the Appalachian Mountains and the Mississippi River. However, the British did not consult the American Indians who had been allied to them during the war. Some of the American Indians made treaties with the United States, but others resisted American settlement. This resistance often had British support and backing. The resulting tensions contributed to the War of 1812 between the United States and Great Britain.

American diplomats Benjamin Franklin, John Adams, Henry Laurens, and John Jay signed the Treaty of Paris on the country's behalf.

The U.S. Constitution

In 1787, the Constitutional Convention was held in Philadelphia to discuss the kind of government the new country should have. As a result of the convention, the U.S. Constitution was drawn up. This document set the rules under which the country would be governed. It laid forth the structure of the U.S. government, creating a strong federal

The U.S. Constitution was signed on September 17, 1787, at the Pennsylvania State House in Philadelphia. Today, this building is called Independence Hall.

system made up of three branches—the executive, the legislative, and the judiciary. The Constitution also put in place a series of checks and balances to make sure that no branch ever had too much power. James Madison, who later served as president, worked hard to create the Bill of Rights. These 10 amendments, outlining the basic rights and freedoms of all Americans, officially became part of the Constitution in 1791.

International Impact

The rebellion against Great Britain had an influence far beyond the shores of North America. Events in the United States had shown how people could overthrow an oppressive and unfair government. The U.S. Constitution proved that ideas about basic rights, such as liberty, equality, and freedom of worship, could actually become reality. As a result of the American Revolutionary War, the United States was now a **democracy**.

This was very different from Europe, where most countries were still ruled by monarchs and the people had very little freedom. The American Revolutionary War had great influence on those who overthrew the monarchy in France. The French Revolution then led to revolutions in other countries throughout the 19th century. In all cases, ordinary citizens took up arms to fight for their rights over what was considered **autocratic rule**.

Public executions were common during the French Revolution. It is estimated that between 16,000 and 40,000 people died by guillotine.

By The Numbers

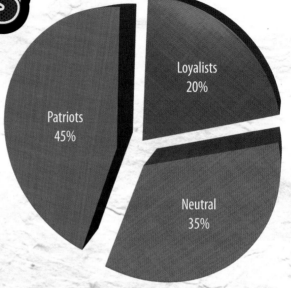

Support for the War

It is often assumed that the Revolutionary War had two sides. People either supported the American fight for independence or stayed loyal to the British. What is rarely mentioned is the fact that a large number of people tried to stay neutral during the war, not taking either side.

Patriots 45%

Loyalists 20%

Neutral 35%

African Americans in the War

There were approximately 3.5 million people living in the colonies during the Revolutionary War. About 5.7 percent of these people enlisted to fight on the American side. An even smaller percentage were African American.

Enlisted African American Patriot Soldiers
5,000

Enlisted African American Loyalist Soldiers
20,000

American Losses

Estimates put American deaths at approximately 40,000 as a result of the war. The majority of American soldiers did not die in battle. Most died from diseases caused by poor sanitary conditions in the field. Others died from wounds received in battle. Many died after they were captured by the British and made prisoners of war.

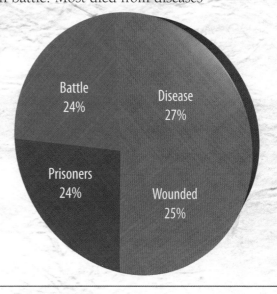

Battle 24%

Disease 27%

Prisoners 24%

Wounded 25%

The Cost of War

The war was very expensive for the Americans. The government had to borrow money from European countries to fund the war effort. The war was expensive for Great Britain and France as well. All countries had to rebuild financially in the years following the war.

= £5 million

= $5 million

States/Colonies Spending
$114 million

Great Britain Spending
£80 million

France Spending
£56 million

American Nation Spending
$37 million

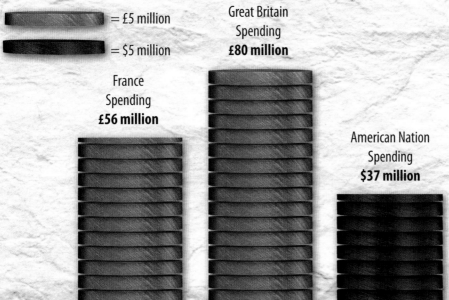

Casualties of War

There were more than 50 separate battles over the course of the American Revolutionary War. Some battles were larger than others, requiring many men and weapons. Each battle, no matter the size, had its share of casualties. At least 6,800 Americans lost their lives on the battlefield. This number was similarly high on the British side. This map highlights some of the American Revolutionary War's key battles, detailing the strength of the American forces and the losses experienced while fighting for independence.

NEW SPAIN

	Conflict	Force	Wounded	Killed	Captured
1.	Trenton	2,400	5	2	0
2.	Yorktown	20,600	180	72	0
3.	Guilford Courthouse	4,400	185	79	75
4.	Cowpens	1,912	124	25	0
5.	Saratoga	9,000	260	60	0
6.	Bunker Hill	2,400	305	115	30
7.	Lexington and Concord	3,800	39	49	0
8.	Princeton	4,500	40	25	0
9.	Brandywine	14,600	600	300	400
10	Kings Mountain	900	58	29	0
	Totals	**64,512**	**1,796**	**756**	**505**

BRITISH COLONIES

NEW HAMPSHIRE

Saratoga, 1777 ⭐5

Concord, 1775

NEW YORK

Lexington, 1775

⭐7 ⭐6 Bunker Hill, 1775

⭐ **MASSACHUSETTS**

⭐ Boston

RHODE ISLAND

CONNECTICUT

Trenton, 1776 ⭐1 ⭐8 Princeton, 1777

PENNSYLVANIA

⭐ **NEW JERSEY**

Brandywine, 1777 ⭐9

DELAWARE

MARYLAND

VIRGINIA

Yorktown, 1781 ⭐2

Guilford Courthouse, 1781

Cowpens, 1781 ⭐3 **NORTH CAROLINA**

⭐4 ⭐10 Kings Mountain, 1780

SOUTH CAROLINA

GEORGIA

WEST FLORIDA

EAST FLORIDA

Legend

🚢 British Blockade

☆ American Victory

⭐ British Victory

• City

⬛ British Colonies

⬜ New Spain

⬜ Unclaimed Land

0   500 Miles

0   500 Kilometers

How We Remember

Many soldiers lost their lives fighting for independence in the American Revolutionary War. Others returned home wounded. The war affected people all over the country. People wanted to honor those who had fought, those who had been injured, and those who had died throughout the course of the war.

TOMB OF THE UNKNOWN REVOLUTIONARY WAR SOLDIER

The Tomb of the Unknown Revolutionary War Soldier is located in Washington Square, a park in central Philadelphia. The monument is dedicated to soldiers who died during the Revolutionary War. Many American and British soldiers were buried in mass graves in the park. In 1954, the decision was made to build a fitting monument to those who died in the war. The memorial was completed in 1957. Archaeologists later located one of the mass graves, and one of the bodies was reburied as the Unknown Soldier. The tomb features the inscription "Beneath this stone rests a soldier of Washington's army who died to give you liberty."

BUNKER HILL MONUMENT

The Bunker Hill Monument honors those who died in the Battle of Bunker Hill in 1775. The monument is located in Boston National Historical Park in Charlestown, Massachusetts. The first memorial on the site was built in 1794 to honor Joseph Warren, a Boston leader who was killed in the battle. Later, it was decided that a memorial for all those who had died at Bunker Hill would be built. The current monument was built between 1827 and 1842. It is a 221-foot (67 m) tall granite **obelisk**. In front of the monument is a statue of William Prescott, one of the American commanders at the battle.

KINGS MOUNTAIN U.S. MONUMENT

The Kings Mountain U.S. Monument is located in the Kings Mountain National Military Park in Blacksburg, South Carolina. It commemorates those who died at the Battle of Kings Mountain in 1780. The monument is an 83-foot (25.3 m) tall obelisk. Bronze tablets rest on each side of the monument. The first tablet describes the Patriot victory, and the second describes the significance of the battle to the outcome of the war. The third tablet lists the commanders on both sides, and the fourth tablet lists the Americans killed in the fighting. The sides of the monument feature sculptures representing victory, peace, and immortality.

Memorials and other symbols of remembrance began to appear across the country in the decades after the war. Some were local monuments, developed by individual communities. Others were created on behalf of the entire country. Today, these memorials and symbols continue to pay tribute to those who served in the Revolutionary War.

MONUMENT TO THE ALLIANCE AND VICTORY

The Monument to the Alliance and Victory is located in Yorktown, Virginia. The monument pays tribute to those who died during the 1781 battle that brought the Revolutionary War to a close. The U.S. Congress authorized the monument immediately after the battle, but construction did not begin for 100 years and was not completed until 1884. The granite column is 84 feet (25.6 m) in height and is capped with a statue of Liberty. The base of the statue has four inscriptions. These inscriptions describe the alliance with France, the British surrender, the terms of the Treaty of Paris, and the history behind the monument's creation.

GUILFORD COURTHOUSE NATIONAL MILITARY PARK

The Guilford Courthouse National Military Park is located in Greensboro, North Carolina. The preserved battlefield has 28 monuments that honor heroes of the Revolutionary War and those who died at the Battle of Guilford Courthouse in March 1781. It was first decided to build a monument in the area to honor Nathanael Greene in the 1850s, but work was interrupted by the Civil War. Work eventually began again in the early 20th century. The monument is a statue of Greene on a horse. In front of the pedestal is a small statue of the Greek goddess Athena holding a shield and laurel leaves.

SARATOGA MONUMENT

The Saratoga Monument is located in Saratoga National Historic Park in New York. The monument commemorates the Battle of Saratoga that took place in October 1777. It is a granite obelisk that is 155 feet (47 m) tall. At the base of the monument are four **niches** that were built to honor the battle's American commanders. The niches feature statues of Philip Schuyler, Daniel Morgan, and Horatio Gates. One niche remains empty. It represents Benedict Arnold, who was part of the American campaign at Saratoga, but later became a traitor to the American cause and joined the British forces.

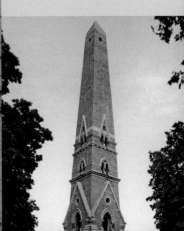

Test Yourself

MIX 'n MATCH

1. Nathanael Greene
2. Henry Knox
3. Constitutional Convention
4. Hessians
5. Boston Tea Party
6. Continental
7. Battle of Yorktown

a. British East India Company
b. Germany
c. Commander of the South
d. Virginia
e. American money
f. Secretary of state for war
g. Philadelphia

TRUE OR FALSE

1. George Washington became commander-in-chief of the Continental Army in 1775.

2. Daniel Morgan was taken prisoner after the Battle of Bunker Hill.

3. The Tomb of the Unknown Revolutionary War Soldier is in Washington, DC.

4. In 1763, a Royal Proclamation prevented Americans from settling west of the Appalachians.

5. Muskets were very accurate and had a range of more than 100 yards (91.4 m).

6. The first Continental Army uniforms were brown.

7. The Treaty of Paris was signed on July 4, 1776.

8. George Washington personally fired the first American shot at the Battle of Yorktown.

MULTIPLE CHOICE

1. Who signed the Treaty of Paris on behalf of the United States?
   a. George Washington, Henry Knox, Daniel Morgan, and Nathanael Greene
   b. Henry Knox, John Adams, George Washington, and Henry Laurens
   c. Benjamin Franklin, John Adams, Henry Laurens, and John Jay
   d. George Washington, Benjamin Franklin, Henry Knox, and John Jay

2. Approximately how many African Americans fought for the American side?
   a. 2,000
   b. 5,000
   c. 10,000
   d. 20,000

3. Where was George Washington born?
   a. Westmoreland County, Virginia
   b. Philadelphia, Pennsylvania
   c. Boston, Massachusetts
   d. Mount Vernon, Virginia

4. When were the Townshend Revenue Acts introduced?
   a. 1773
   b. 1771
   c. 1769
   d. 1767

5. How many British soldiers surrendered at Yorktown?
   a. More than 8,000
   b. Approximately 5,000
   c. More than 12,000
   d. Approximately 900

6. Approximately how many soldiers did it take to operate a cannon?
   a. 10
   b. 4
   c. 14
   d. 8

7. Who was the British commander at the Battle of Saratoga?
   a. General Thomas Gage
   b. General John Burgoyne
   c. General Charles Cornwallis
   d. General William Howe

Key Words

ally: a country, group, or person in an alliance with another

artillery: large guns used by an army, or the troops that use them

autocratic rule: government by a single person having unlimited power

blockaded: isolated an area, usually a port, by ships to prevent entry and exit

boycotting: refusing to buy or use something as a means of protest

casualties: people who have been killed, wounded, taken prisoner, or gone missing in action

cavalry: a section of an army that fights on horseback

civilians: people who are not members of the military

colonial rule: when a nation maintains or extends its control over foreign dependencies

colonies: areas under the full or partial political control of another country

Constitutional Convention: the 1787 meeting at which delegates drafted the U.S. Constitution

democracy: a form of government in which the supreme power is vested in the people and exercised directly by them or their elected representatives

dictators: people who rule absolutely and oppressively

Enlightenment: an 18th-century philosophical movement

French and Indian War: a war between France and Great Britain that took place in North America and lasted from 1755 to 1761

garrison: the troops stationed in a fortress or town to defend it

Hessians: German soldiers who fought for Great Britain in the American Revolutionary War

infantry: an army consisting of soldiers who fight on foot

inflation: a persistent increase in prices or a similar decline in the value of money

Loyalist: an American colonist who remained loyal to Great Britain during the war

militia: a fighting force made up of non-professional soldiers

monopoly: exclusive control of the buying or selling of a product or service

niches: recesses in walls meant to house statues

obelisk: a tall, four-sided shaft of stone that has a pointed pyramid on the top

Patriot: an American who supported independence from Great Britain

reconnaissance: the process of obtaining information about the position of the enemy

revenues: the income a government receives from taxes, customs charges, and excise duties

siege: when an army surrounds a city, town, or fortress in an attempt to capture it

snipers: soldiers who shoot at others from a concealed location

treaty: a document between two or more countries to agree to cooperate on certain matters. A treaty is also signed to agree on peace terms after a war is over.

Index

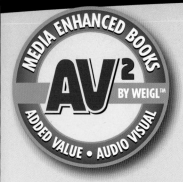

Log on to www.av2books.com

AV² by Weigl brings you media enhanced books that support active learning. Go to www.av2books.com, and enter the special code found on page 2 of this book. You will gain access to enriched and enhanced content that supplements and complements this book. Content includes video, audio, weblinks, quizzes, a slide show, and activities.

AV² Online Navigation

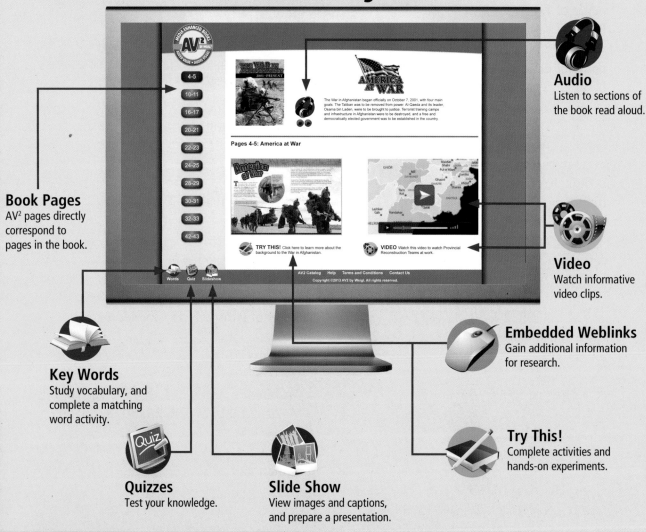

Audio
Listen to sections of the book read aloud.

Book Pages
AV² pages directly correspond to pages in the book.

Video
Watch informative video clips.

Key Words
Study vocabulary, and complete a matching word activity.

Embedded Weblinks
Gain additional information for research.

Quizzes
Test your knowledge.

Slide Show
View images and captions, and prepare a presentation.

Try This!
Complete activities and hands-on experiments.

AV² was built to bridge the gap between print and digital. We encourage you to tell us what you like and what you want to see in the future.

Sign up to be an AV² Ambassador at www.av2books.com/ambassador.

Due to the dynamic nature of the Internet, some of the URLs and activities provided as part of AV² by Weigl may have changed or ceased to exist. AV² by Weigl accepts no responsibility for any such changes. All media enhanced books are regularly monitored to update addresses and sites in a timely manner. Contact AV² by Weigl at 1-866-649-3445 or av2books@weigl.com with any questions, comments, or feedback.